Ice Bear and Little Fox

by **Jonathan London**

paintings by **Daniel San Souci**

SCHOLASTIC INC.

New York Toronto London Auckland Sydney
Mexico City New Delhi Hong Kong

Glossary

aglu Inuit, or Eskimo, word for a snow cave

ah-tik-tok Inuit name for a polar cub in its learning stage, meaning "those who go down to the sea"

auk black-and-white diving seabird that breeds in colder parts of the North

berg floating mass of ice from a glacier or polar ice sheet. Only one-ninth of a berg is seen above water.

floe large, floating sheet of ice formed across the surface of a body of water

heath low, shrubby evergreen plants having needle-like leaves and clusters of small flowers

kelp large brown seaweed that is a vital source of food for marine animals

kittiwake long-winged, web-footed seagull inhabiting the North Atlantic

lemming small, short-tailed, furry-footed rodent related to the meadow mouse

lichen plant made up of algae and fungus growing upon a solid surface, such as a rock. Lichens are an important food source for many Arctic animals.

mussel dark, long, and narrow shellfish

nanuq Inuit name for the polar bear

narwhal Arctic aquatic mammal with a large head and paddle-shaped forelimbs. The male has a long, twisted ivory tusk, which is actually a modified tooth, and is believed by many to be the origin of the legendary unicorn.

netsik Inuit name for the seal

Northern Lights streamers and arches of light stretched across the night sky, which appear in the Arctic regions; also known as aurora borealis

orca killer whale

P Inuit name for the polar bear, meaning "the great wanderer"

ptarmigan type of grouse with plumage that changes color each season to match the environment, and feet covered with feathers to serve as snowshoes

teeguk Inuit name for an old bull seal

tiriganniaq Inuit name for the Arctic fox

tundra treeless plains of the Arctic and subarctic regions

vole small rodent closely related to muskrats and lemmings, but resembling a stocky mouse or rat

ISBN 0-439-16159-2

Designed by Richard Amari

Text copyright © 1998 by Jonathan London. Illustrations copyright © 1998 by Daniel San Souci. All rights reserved. Published by Scholastic Inc., 555 Broadway, New York, NY 10012, by arrangement with Dutton Children's Books, a division of Penguin Putnam Inc. SCHOLASTIC and associated logos are trademarks and/or registered trademarks of Scholastic Inc.

12 11 10 9 8 7 6 5 4 3 2   0 1 2 3 4 5/0

Printed in the U.S.A.   14

First Scholastic printing, January 2000

Z702036   R702   2/01

On a still, midwinter night,
when the Northern Lights blaze
in glowing curtains of fire,
a young bear climbs a berg.
Rearing up on his hind legs,
he tastes the air.

Nanuq the Ice Bear
is spending his first year
away from his mother.
He slides down the steep slope
to the jumble of ice below.
Somewhere behind him,
something follows.

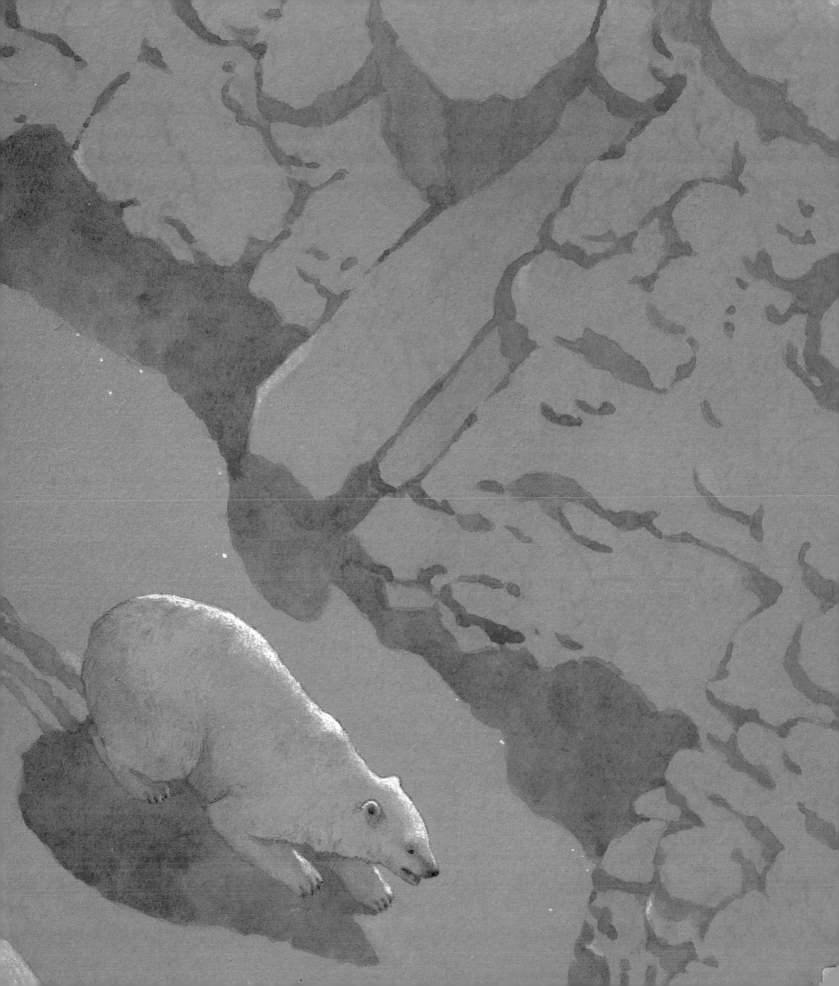

It is an Arctic fox,
white and ghostlike
in the low moon.

All around them, the ice crackles
and buckles into great ridges.
Bergs groan and growl
and rumble like thunder.
Then the sound dies away
to a sudden stillness.

Underneath the ice and snow,
Netsik the Seal swims into his *aglu*,
his snow cave.

Somewhere up above,
Nanuq hears the muffled tinkle of
water beneath the mound of white.

He pauses, his body poised,
ears twitching.

Then suddenly he lunges,
slamming through the snow roof
on all fours...

and lands crashing on his prey.

Little Fox waits
at a respectful distance.
He will eat what Ice Bear leaves.

All through the long dark of winter,
as the moon circles low in the sky,
Ice Bear wanders,
scouting for *Netsik's* lair.
And wherever Ice Bear goes,
Little Fox follows.

By mid-May, the first hints
of summer come to the Arctic.
The first green in the heath
breaks through the snow.
The first brown feathers show
in the ptarmigan's white plumage.
Soon Little Fox, too, will turn brown.

The sun has returned,
and on the broken slabs of sea ice,
the snow caves melt.
From now on, Ice Bear hunts
at *Netsik's* breathing holes.

Downwind, he waits and waits,
flat to the ice—his patience matched
by the young fox, who curls up
in a hollow scooped out of snow.
Floes crack, hours pass.

Suddenly, *Teeguk,* an old bull seal,
pokes his head up through the
hole…and *Nanuq* the Ice Bear
strikes like lightning.

His stomach filled,
Ice Bear wanders off,
rolls on his back,
and waves all four legs in the air.
While Ice Bear dallies in the sun,
Little Fox nibbles on the leftovers.

By late June, the meadows are
bright with purple and yellow flowers.
Ice Bear feasts
on early tundra berries,
grazes on grass, lichens, and moss.
Little Fox pounces nearby
on lemmings and voles.

But it is the sea that calls to *Nanuq*,
the Ice Bear, the Sea Bear.
He dives for mussels and kelp.
He strokes and glides,
turns and rolls like an otter,
then soundlessly rises for air.

But the sea in summer is dangerous.
A bear is no match in the sea
for a bull walrus with
his huge tusks.
But there is something else.
Something worse.
Little Fox barks a warning
and Ice Bear looks.

It's the killer whales, the orcas!
They come slicing through
the dark water,
chasing a pair of narwhals,
whose long horns flash,
then sink away, side by side.

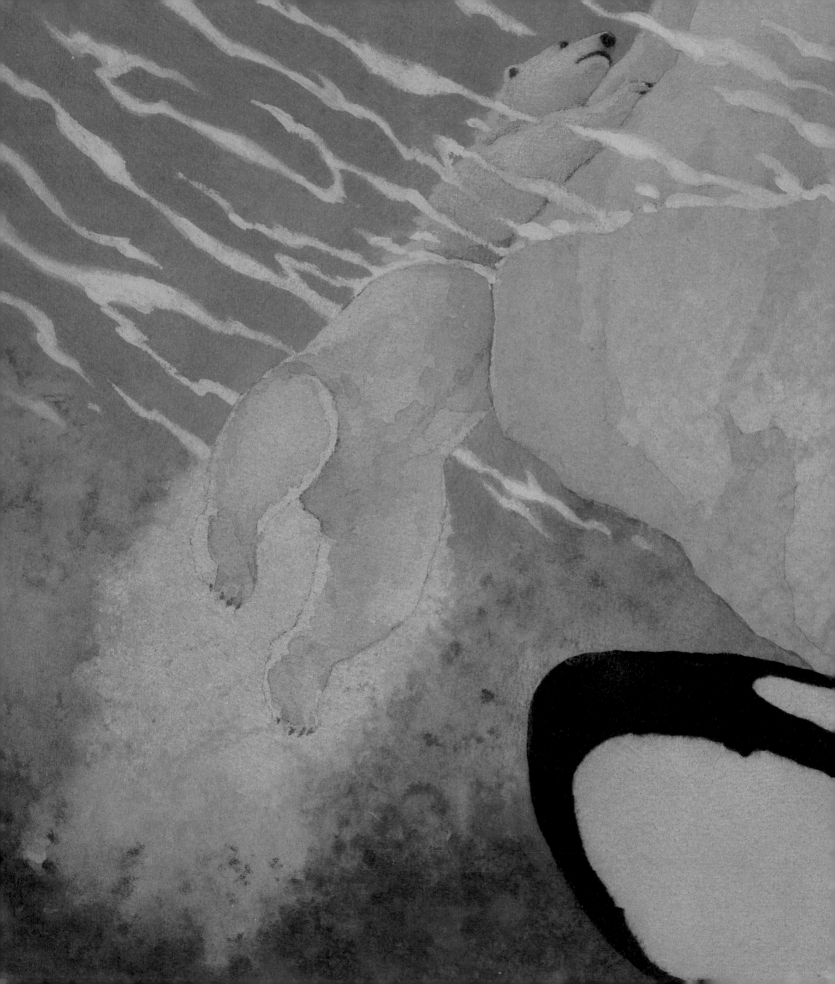

The killer whales pivot…
and turn toward *Nanuq*!
Frantic, he claws at a floe
and hauls himself up.
From below, the hunters smash
against the ice with their backs.
It bucks and cracks.
It heaves and jerks and sways.
Then Ice Bear leaps…

and lands on the rock shore
of Little Fox's island.

Nanuq shakes off like a great dog
and stops to gaze at the little one
who had warned him
of great danger.

Little Fox—his fur now almost
the brown of the earth—
taps the air with his nose.
Then he circles once and sits,
facing the great white bear,
letting his tongue slide in and out
between his small, sharp teeth.

All summer, Ice Bear rafts on floes,
sails on bergs,
from island to island.
But Little Fox stays behind,
wary of the open sea and
the danger there.
He will hunt for hares
and lemmings,
and later, maybe a mate.

With the coming of winter,
the sea ice closes in.
The gulls, auks, and kittiwakes
disappear to the south,
and the polar night begins again
in deep silence.

And somewhere in that
wilderness of ice,
Little Fox rejoins Ice Bear.
But now there are two
hungry foxes, mates for life,
trotting behind *Nanuq,*
forever following, keeping watch
in the long night.

Afterword

ICE BEAR, Ice King, Sea Bear, Great White Bear—*Nanuq*. All are powerful names for polar bears. Considered the largest land carnivores, or meat-eaters, in the world, they are matched in size only by the Kodiak brown bear. Twice as big as a lion or tiger, a large male polar bear can stand twelve feet tall and weigh two thousand pounds. With one swipe of his huge paw, he could flip a four-hundred-pound seal into the air.

The young cubs are the size of guinea pigs when they are born. Later, in their learning stage, the cubs are called by some Eskimos, or Inuit, *ah-tik-tok*: "those who go down to the sea." Their mothers then teach them how to catch seals, which make up more than 90 percent of a polar bear's diet.

Polar Eskimos of northwest Greenland call an ice bear *pisugtooq*: "the great wanderer." Always in search of the best places to hunt seals, *pisugtooq* may even be seen swimming hundreds of miles out at sea. A sea bear can eat one hundred pounds of seal blubber in one meal.

In the Arctic, the sun does not rise in the winter or set in the summer. The hollow, transparent hairs of a polar bear's coat allow sunlight to reach and warm the bear's black skin. In winter, the thick layer of fat underneath the skin helps keep the bear warm.

Young ice bears usually follow their mothers for two and a half years. (By then, a male bear is larger than his mother.) It's at this point—when the young bears are on their own for the first time—that they are at highest risk. Their survival hinges on learning to live alone. If a young polar bear survives the first couple of years living alone, it is usually ready to mate by four or five years of age. After mating, the bears will once again go their different ways.

But polar bears are not always truly alone. They are often followed by one or more Arctic foxes, called *tiriganniaq* by the Inuit. Especially in winter, these friendliest and most trusting of North American foxes tag along with ice bears, hungry for leftovers.

Weighing only six to ten pounds, these small foxes also hunt for birds and rodents. Lemmings are among their favorite prey. Foxes have such good ears that they can hear a lemming running underground through its burrow. But hunting takes a lot of energy. Eating an ice bear's leftovers is often easier.

The male is called a dog fox and will link up with a female, a vixen, anytime after it is six months old. Foxes mate for life.

Not only have Arctic foxes been watching ice bears for thousands of years, but so have Eskimos. Eskimos probably learned their seal-hunting techniques by watching polar bears hunt. Ice bears are essential to the traditional Eskimo way of life and are an integral part of Inuit culture and legend.

We can all learn from *Nanuq* the Ice Bear about surviving with dignity, and from *Tiriganniaq* the Little Fox about living with our neighbors, even in the harshest place on earth.